Paul
innocent

The Bible On
Suffering

The Bible

on

Suffering

by A. BERTRANGS

Translated by F. Vander Heijden

ST. NORBERT ABBEY PRESS
De Pere, Wisconsin
U. S. A.
1966

Originally published as
De Bijbel over het Lijden
Roermond and Maaseik, J. J. Romen & Zonen, 1962

Library of Congress catalogue card number: 66 - 16990

Printed in the United States of America
ST. NORBERT ABBEY PRESS
De Pere, Wisconsin

CONTENTS

FOREWORD

When we read the sacred authors in connection with the problem of suffering we soon realize that the Old and the New Testament cannot be placed on the same plane. The Old Testament considers it chiefly from the point of view of retribution, while the New Testament looks at it preferably as a problem in itself. One of the reasons for this is that the Old Testament investigates something, while the New above all wishes to demonstrate something. The former occupies itself with the **cause** of suffering, the latter stresses its **meaning.** We can express the same difference in another way: the books of the Old Testament are **struggling** with suffering, those of the New are actually **living** it.

Of course this does not infer that the Old Testament does not understand the meaning of suffering. But it always confines itself to asking questions about its meaning — so much so that we may conclude that it speaks about vexing, rather than about meaningful, suffering.

In this book we will treat the problem and the grace of suffering.

THE PROBLEM OF SUFFERING

In this section we shall treat the cause and the meaning of suffering as found in the Old Testament.

A. WHY SUFFERING?

For the sake of clarity we divide our explanation into two parts: suffering and the growing insight into the problem of retribution; and suffering and the sin of the first man.

1. Suffering and the growing insight into the problem of retribution

The people of Israel believed in divine retribution. This was a consequence of their ethical monotheism and their belief in God as a just judge.

But how did they understand this? For many centuries the Jews did not believe in a retribution hereafter. They believed in a survival of the human person, but this was one which had no appeal. After death man became, as it were, a pale shade and resided in an obscure underworld, in Hebrew called **Sheol,** a place of darkness and silence from which no return was possible, because there were heavy gates which prevented escape.[1] Life in Sheol was attenuated, even deathlike: as Ecclesiastes says (9:10):

"There is no work or thought or knowledge or wisdom in Sheol."[2] It goes without saying that everyone abhorred the place, except those for whom the earth was a vale of tears.[3] All things considered, life in this underworld was exactly the same for the good and the evil: there is no question of any retribution.

But the Jews were convinced that there would be retribution. Since there was no retribution in Sheol, it was bound to take place on earth: happiness was the reward for virtue, unhappiness the punishment for evil. For centuries this was their only theory; they believed only in a purely earthly retribution, collective or individual. It was not until the eve of Christ's coming that they developed a different view, and spoke of an individual retribution which would not take place on earth.

a. Collective retribution on earth

In the initial period of their history, when they were still nomads, as well in the next period, when they had settled, the Jews maintained that the crimes of an individual had to be compensated for by the group to which he belonged, more especially by his next of kin or his descendants or, in the case of a king, by his subjects.[4] This was a direct consequence of their deep respect for the bonds connecting a group, without which it would have been impossible for them to maintain themselves and to prosper.

They held the same opinions in religious matters. Rules which were in vogue in their social life were also applied to God's dealing with a sinful people.

Thus we read in Ex. 20:5: "I, Yahweh your God am a jealous God, visiting the iniquity of the fathers upon the children to the third and the fourth generation of those who hate me!"

However, the principle of collective retribution was more than once found to be out of accord with the facts. Reaction was inevitable. Why did the pious king Josiah have to die young and even on the field of battle (2 Chron. 25:20-21)? Why did Yahweh punish Juda, relatively not so bad, while Babylon remained unharmed (Hab. 1:13)?

The conservatives of that day fought to maintain the principle. They held to considerations such as these: When Yahweh rewards, he treats people according to the rule of solidarity, more so than when he punishes (Ex. 20:6); a small number of just people is sufficient to save a guilty town (Gen. 18:22-33); punishment visited upon a majority admits of exceptions (Jer. 45).

However all did not accept the arguments. In the days of Jeremiah and Ezekiel critical minds spread the following satiric ditty: "The fathers have eaten sour grapes, and the children's teeth are set on edge" (Jer. 31:29; Ezek. 18:2).

b. Individual retribution on earth

Yahweh ordered Ezekiel to put an end to this theory. Everyone is rewarded for his own good deeds and is punished for his own sins:

"The word of Yahweh came to me again: What

do you mean by repeating this proverb concerning the land of Israel: The fathers have eaten sour grapes, and the children's teeth are set on edge? As I live says the Lord Yahweh, this proverb shall not more be used by you in Israel. Behold, all souls are mine; the soul of the father as well as the soul of the son is mine; the soul that sins shall die.

If a man is righteous and does what is lawful and right — if he does not eat upon the mountains or lift up his eyes to the idols of the house of Israel, does not defile his neighbor's wife or approach a woman in her time of impurity, does not oppress any one, but restores to the debtor his pledge, commits no robbery, gives his bread to the hungry and covers the naked with a garment, does not lend at interest or take any increase, withholds his hand upon iniquity, executes true justice between man and man, walks in my statutes, and is careful to observe my ordinances — he is righteous, he shall surely live, says the Lord Yahweh.

If he begets a son who is a robber, a shedder of blood, who does none of these duties, but eats upon the mountains, defiles his neighbor's wife, oppresses the poor and needy, commits robbery, does not restore the pledge, lifts up his eyes to the idols, commits abomination, lends at interest, and takes increase; shall he then live? He shall not live. He has done all these abominable things; he shall surely die; his blood shall be upon himself.

But if this man begets a son who sees all the sins

which his father has done, and fears, and does not do likewise, who does not eat upon the mountains or lift up his eyes to the idols of the house of Israel, does not defile his neighbor's wife, does not wrong any one, exacts no pledge, commits no robbery, but gives his bread to the hungry and covers the naked with a garment, withholds his hand from iniquity, takes no interest or increase, observes my ordinances, and walks in my statutes; he shall not die for his father's iniquity; he shall surely live. As for his father, because he practiced extortion, robbed his brother, and did what is not good among his people, behold, he shall die for his iniquity.

Yet you say: Why should not the son suffer for the iniquity of his father? When the son has done what is lawful and right, and has been careful to observe all my statutes, he shall surely live. The soul that sins shall die. The son shall not suffer for the iniquity of his father, nor the father suffer for the iniquity of the son; the righteousness of the righteous shall be upon himself, and the wickedness of the wicked shall be upon himself.

But if a wicked man turns away from all his sins which he has committed and keeps all my statutes and does what is lawful and right, he shall surely live; he shall not die. None of the transgressions which he has committed shall be remembered against him; for the righteousness which he has done he shall live. Have I any pleasure in the death of the wicked, says the Lord Yahweh, and not rather that he should turn from his way and live?

But when a righteous man turns away from his righteousness and commits iniquity and does the same abominable things that the wicked man does, will he live? None of the righteous deeds which he has done shall be remembered; for the treachery of which he is guilty and the sin he has committed, he shall die.

Yet you say: The way of the Lord is not just. Hear now, O house of Israel: Is my way not just? When a righteous man turns away from his righteousness and commits iniquity, he shall die for it; for the iniquity which he has committed he shall die. Again, when a wicked man turns away from the wickedness he has committed and does what is lawful and right, he shall save his life. Because he considered and turned away from all the transgressions which he had committed, he shall surely live, he shall not die" (Ezek. 18:1-28).

The time was ripe for this doctrine of Ezekiel. The nation as such no longer existed, because it had lost its independence and lived in exile. There was no way of rebuilding hope for a better future except on the displaced individuals. For this reason each one of them was admonished to repent: "Therefore I will judge you, every one according to his ways" (Ezek. 18:30). But retribution was still regarded as having to occur on earth. Wealth, success, honor, peace, a long life, a numerous progeny were considered the reward of a pious man (Ps. 128; cf. Ps. 112; 127). He who kept the law of Yahweh, would prosper in all his undertakings (Ps. 1:3). The op-

ponents of Job were relying on tradition and experience when they said: "Think now, who that was
innocent ever perished? Or where were the upright
cut off? As I have seen, those who plow iniquity and
sow trouble reap the same!"⁵

Once again theory and fact seemed to clash. An
unknown poet attacked this current opinion. On
a popular story, in which this current doctrine was
held, he grafted, about 500 B.C., a dispute between
a few conservatives and the man Job. Boldly and
incisively he made Job state his grievances, with the
sole intent of finding a solution worthy of God and
of man in the case of a pious person who suffers:

> Why do the wicked live,
> reach old age, and grow mighty in power?
> Their children are established in their presence,
> and their offspring before their eyes.
> Their houses are safe from fear,
> and no rod of God is upon them.
> Their bull breeds without fail;
> their cow calves, and does not cast her calf.
> They send forth their little ones like a flock,
> and their children dance.
> They sing to the tambourine and the lyre,
> and rejoice to the sound of the pipe.
> They spend their days in prosperity,
> and in peace they go down to the Sheol.
> They say to God: Depart from us!
> We do not desire the knowledge of thy ways.
> What is the Almighty, that we should serve him?
> And what profits do we get if we pray to him?
> (21:7-15)

Did the author of Job find an answer to the
question: Why suffering? An exact explanation of
Job 19:25-27 will enable us to answer.

The Hebrew text has not been handed down to
us undamaged. Hence every translation must attempt
a reconstruction and must be hypothetical. Consequently, translations differ — so much so that a
reader asks himself: Which interpretation best ap-
proaches the possible wording and the probable
thought of Job? Since this is not the place for a
technical exposition of this topic we should offer no
apology for the translation we propose.

In certain versions of Job 19:25 we read: "For I
know that my Redeemer lives, and at last he will
stand upon the earth." The words "Redeemer," "at
last" and "stand upon the earth" at once turn our
attention toward Christ's return at the end of time,
even though the translator, as sometimes happens,
points out in a footnote, that this meaning is not
intended. We also think at once of the resurrection
of the dead, but there is question as to whether Job
himself was thinking of this. Our impression may
be even more vivid when we read in 19:26: "After
my skin has been thus destroyed, then from my flesh
I shall see God."

We propose to translate as follows:

"For I know that my Defender lives and will stand
upon the earth to have the last word:

After they have harassed my skin and I have become a skeleton, I shall see God;

I shall see him, taking my side entirely; my eyes
will see him, but not as my enemy.
My kidneys within me long for that."

As regards verse 25 ("For I . . . the last word"),
"Defender" cannot mean anything but a defender in
a law suit. This is exactly where Job finds himself.
In the first place he is involved in a suit against God,
who has taken away from him everything he had:
"That he would maintain the right of a man with
God" (16:21). He therefore needs a lawyer or a
witness for the defense: sometimes this is his blood,
at other times his cry for help (16:18-20). We should
remember that in the biblical milieu the blood of
man who is unjustly killed or wounded calls to God
for vengeance as long as it is not covered up with
earth. Thus God says to Cain: "The voice of your
brother's blood is crying to me from the ground."[6]
An oppressed man's cry for help is seen as standing
before God's throne as his defendant; thus a psalmist
prays: "Hear my prayer, O Yahweh; let my cry come
to thee!"[7] At the same time Job is involved in a case
against three so-called friends, who consider his
misfortune a punishment from heaven and consequently accuse him of impiety: "Think now, who
that was innocent ever perished? Or where were
the upright cut off? As I have seen, those who plow
iniquity and sow trouble reap the same" (4:7-8). In
this case God himself is Job's defender. Contrary
to the situation as it was before, God now is not
his adversary, but his advocate; therefore we must
notice the shift which has taken place in the situa-

tion. However fiercely Job's accusers plead against him, God will subsequently enter into the case and will speak the last word: Job will be acquitted! Consequently he will be reinstated on earth in his former affluence; whatever has been taken from him will be given back.

In verse 26 ("After they have . . . I shall see God") we are told that his flesh has already shrunken away under the attack of his accusers; only his skin is left, but they want this too. They will, however, not get it, because at the last moment God will intercede for him.[8]

Does 19:25-27 mean that Job believed in a resurrection?

The Latin translator thought so. His version is well known from the liturgy of the dead: "Because I know that my Redeemer lives and on the last day I shall rise from the earth; and I shall be vested with my skin again and in my flesh I shall see God!"

The opposite opinion, however, is more probable.

In the first place, because of the context, we must say that the author of Job was of the opinion that no escape from Sheol was possible. Repeatedly he says: "He who goes down to Sheol does not come up."[9] And what he says in 14:13-14 does not contradict this: "Oh that thou wouldest hide me in Sheol, that thou wouldest conceal me until thy wrath be past, that thou wouldest appoint me a set time, and remember me! If a man die shall he live again?" That

this however does not mean a hidden hope for resurrection, not **a hoping against all hope,** but really is
a case of wishful thinking, we can see from what
Job says in other verses: "But man dies, and is laid
low; man breathes his last, and where is he? As
waters fail from a lake, and a river wastes away and
dries up, so man lies down and rises not again; till
the heavens are no more he will not awake, or be
roused out of his sleep" (verses 10-12); and further
on: "But the mountain falls and crumbles away, and
the rock is removed from its place; the waters wear
away the stones; the torrents wash away the soil of
the earth; so thou destroyest the hope of man till the
heavens are no more he will not awake, or be roused
out of his sleep" (verses 18-19 and 12b).

In the second place we may point out what the
author thinks about retribution. He appears to be
a child of his time in this matter. The abode of the
dead does not offer any chance for a just retribution,
because the good and the evil equally suffer the
same mournful lot. No one therefore wishes to go
to this place of silence from which no return is
possible, except those who had to suffer very much
on earth and for whom death is a liberation.[10] Yet
somewhere there must be a retribution, because after
all God is just. This therefore can only be on earth.
In the sight of his tribulations Job clings desperately
to this hope, and against all appearances professes
his confidence in God's retribution: "For I know that
my Defender lives and will stand upon the earth to
have the last word. My kidneys within me long for
that."

No, the author of Job did not at all know the Christian truths of the resurrection of the body and of the beatific vision of God in heaven. But this is no cause for concern: the Christian knows that the Bible elsewhere has other and very clear texts regarding these truths.

One might feel disappointed that he saw no solution for the problem of suffering except humble acceptance of God's mysterious will. But is "disappointed" the real word? Indeed is sincere subjection to God's will not the kernel of any other solution? And is not Job spiritually related to Christ, who once prayed: "My father, if it be possible, let this cup pass from me; nevertheless, not as I will, but as thou wilt?"

The splendor which breaks through the night of Job's anguish and doubt is his unshakeable faith in his just and provident God: "I know that my Defender lives." And surely Christ meant the same when he said: "Fear not, little flock, for it is your Father's good pleasure to give you the kingdom" (Lk. 12:32).

Ecclesiastes, about 200 B.C., also occupied itself with this problem. But unlike Job this author was not torn by interior anguish; he neither suffered nor hoped as Job did. He simply places his finger upon the wound, without looking for a solution: "There is a vanity which takes place on earth, that there are righteous men to whom it happens according to the deeds of the wicked, and there are wicked men to whom it happens according to the deeds of the righteous. I said that this also is vanity" (8:14; cf. 7:15; 8:10).

One might expect that the stand of Job and Ecclesiastes would have destroyed the current opinion. But this is not so. Jesus, son of Sirach, a bourgeois and a conservative in the 2nd century B.C., still defends the old view (Sir. 16).

c. Individual retribution hereafter

The case of the pious man who lives in misery or who at least is less well off than the sinner, intrigued several psalmists as it did Job and Ecclesiastes. Psalms 16, 49 and 73 come to mind. We quote them in their entirety because of their importance.

> Preserve me, O God, for in thee I take refuge.
> I say to the Lord: Thou art my Lord; I have no
>   good apart from thee.
> As for the saints in the land, they are the noble,
> in whom is all my delight.
>
> Those who choose another god multiply their
>   sorrows;
> their libations of blood I will not pour out
> or take their name upon my lips.
>
> The Lord is my chosen portion and my cup;
> thou holdest my lot.
> The lines have fallen for me in pleasant places;
> yea, I have a goodly heritage.
>
> I bless the Lord who gives me counsel;
> in the night also my heart instructs me.

I keep the Lord always before me;
because he is at my right hand, I shall not be
    moved.

Therefore my heart is glad, and my soul rejoices;
my body also dwells secure.
For thou dost not give me up to Sheol,
or let thy godly one see the Pit.

Thou dost show me the path of life;
in thy presence there is fullness of joy,
in thy right hand are pleasures for evermore
                        (Ps. 16).

Hear this, all peoples!
Give ear, all inhabitants of the world,
both low and high,
rich and poor together!
My mouth shall speak wisdom;
the meditation of my heart shall be
    understanding.
I will incline my ear to a proverb;
I will solve my riddle to the music of the lyre.

Why should I fear in times of trouble,
when the iniquity of my persecutors surrounds
    me,
men who trust in their wealth
and boast of the abundance of their riches?
Truly no man can ransom himself,
or give to God the price of his life,
for the ransom of his life is costly,
and can never suffice,
that he should continue to live on for ever
and never see the Pit.

Yea, he shall see that even the wise die,
the fool and the stupid alike must perish
and leave their wealth to others.
Their graves are their homes for ever,
their dwelling places to all generations,
though they named lands their own.
Men cannot abide in his pomp,
he is like the beasts that perish.

This is the fate of those who have foolish
    confidence
the end of those who are pleased with their
    portion.
Like sheep they are appointed for Sheol;
Death shall be their shepherd;
straight to the grave they descend,
and their form shall waste away;
Sheol shall be their home.
But God will ransom my soul from the power
    of Sheol,
for he will receive me.

Be not afraid when one becomes rich,
when the glory of his house increases.
For when he dies he will carry nothing away;
his glory will not go down after him.
Though, when he lives, he counts himself happy,
and though a man gets praise when he does well
    for himself,
he will go to the generation of his fathers,
who will never more see the light.
Man cannot abide in his pomp,
he is like the beasts that perish (Ps. 49).

Truly God is good to the upright,
to those who are pure in heart.
But as for me, my feet had almost stumbled,
my steps had well nigh slipped.
For I was envious of the arrogant,
when I saw the prosperity of the wicked.

For they have no pangs;
their bodies are sound and sleek.
They are not in trouble as other men are;
they are not stricken like other men.
Therefore pride is their necklace;
violence covers them as a garment.
Their eyes swell out with fatness,
their hearts overflow with follies.
They scoff and speak with malice;
loftily they threaten oppression.
They set their mouths against the heavens,
and their tongue struts through the earth.

Therefore the people turn and praise them;
and find no fault in them.
And they say: How can God know?
Is there knowledge in the Most High?
Behold, these are the wicked;
always at ease, they increase in riches.
And in vain I have kept my heart clean
and washed my hands in innocence.
For all the day long I have been stricken,
and chastened every morning.

If I had said: I will speak thus,
I would have been untrue to the generation of
    thy children.

But when I thought how to understand this,
it seemed to me a wearisome task,
until I went into the sanctuary of God;
then I perceived their end.
Truly thou dost set them in slippery places;
thou dost make them fall to ruin.
How they are destroyed in a moment,
swept away utterly by terrors!
They are like a dream when one awakes,
on awaking : you despise their phantoms.

When my soul was embittered
when I was pricked in heart,
I was stupid and ignorant,
I was like a beast toward thee.
Nevertheless I am continually with thee;
thou dost hold my right hand.
Thou dost guide me with thy counsel,
and afterward thou wilt receive me to glory.
Whom have I in heaven but thee?
And there is nothing upon earth that I desire
     besides thee.
My flesh and my heart may fail,
but God is my strength the strength of my heart
and my portion for ever.

For lo, those who are far from thee shall perish;
thou dost put an end to those who are false to
     thee.
But for me it is good to be near God;
I have made the Lord God my refuge,
that I may tell of all thy words (Ps. 73).

In several verses we are reminded of the moving
tones of Job:

> For the wicked have no pangs;
> their bodies are sound and sleek.
> They are not in trouble as other men are;
> they are not stricken like other men . . .
> They set their mouths against the heavens,
> and their tongue struts through the earth . . .
> And they say: How can God know?
> is there knowledge in the Most High?
> Behold, these are the wicked;
> always at ease, they increase in riches!
> All in vain I have kept my heart clean
> and washed my hands in innocence.
> For all the day long I have been stricken,
> and chastened every morning
> (73:4-5, 9, 11-12, 13-14).

The psalmists however did not go as far as Job:
they refrained from uttering dissatisfaction and did
not call upon God to answer for himself, because they
knew:

> If I had said: I will speak thus,
> I would have been untrue to the generation of
> thy children (73:15).

If they had indulged in such feeling, the results
would have been still worse. Therefore they deemed
themselves fortunate in being able to control themselves:

> But as for me, my feet had almost stumbled,
> and my steps had well nigh slipped.

> For I was envious of the arrogant,
> when I saw the prosperity of the wicked (73:2-3).

Hence they did not need to ask forgiveness as Job
had done (Job 39: 33-35).

Their standpoint however was not the result of
a quicker intelligence, because in the beginning they
too were astonished:

> But when I thought how to understand this,
> it seemed to me a wearisome task (73:16).[11]

They found consolation in certain considerations
to which Job did not arrive, but which had nothing
to do with the problem of the suffering of a pious
man. What they had in mind was the perishability
of earthly wealth:

> But when I thought how to understand this,
> it seemed to me a wearisome task,
> until I went into the sanctuary of God;
> then I perceived their end[12]
> how they are destroyed in a moment . . .
> like a dream when one awakes (73:16, 17, 19, 20).

They were struck by the insufficiency of wealth:

> Why should I fear in times of trouble,
> when the iniquity of my persecutors surrounds
>   me,
> men who trust in their wealth
> and boast of the abundance of their riches?
> Truly no man can ransom himself,
> or give to God the price of his life;[13]

the ransom of his life is costly (49:6-9).

They were not blind to the dangers connected with wealth:

Truly thou dost set them in slippery places
(73:18; cf. 16:14).

Therefore they tried to get into closer association with God:

When my soul was embittered,
when I was pricked in heart,[14]
I was stupid and ignorant,
I was like a beast toward thee.
Nevertheless I am continually with thee,
thou dost hold my right hand . . .
But for me it is good to be near God;
I have made the Lord God my refuge
(73:21-23, 28).

Preserve me, O God, for in thee I take refuge.
I say to the Lord: Thou art my Lord, I have no
good apart from thee.
I bless the Lord who gives me counsel;
in the night also my heart instructs me.
I keep the Lord always before me;
because he is at my right hand, I shall not be
moved.
Therefore my heart is glad, and my soul rejoices
(16:1-2, 7-8, 9).

Moreover they firmly hoped that Yahweh would save them from Sheol: their personal association with him was so intimate, that they banished from their thoughts every idea of breaking up this association (love tends to be eternal):

> My body dwells secure.
> For thou dost not give me up to Sheol,
> or let the godly one see the Pit.
> Thou dost show me the path of life;
> in thy presence there is fullness of joy,
> in thy right hand are pleasures for evermore
> (16:9-11).

> My flesh and my heart may fail,
> but God is the rock of my heart
> and my portion for ever.
> Thou dost guide me with thy counsel,
> and afterward thou wilt receive me to glory
> (73:26, 24).

They expected the same as an answer from God for their fidelity:

> Truly no man can ransom himself,
> or give to God the price of his life,
> for the ransom of his life is costly
> and can never suffice . . .
> But God will ransom my soul from the power
> of Sheol
> for he will receive me (49:8, 9, 16).

The psalmists, after all, did not get any further than Job did regarding the problem confronting us: neither he nor they considered their sufferings as punishment. Because they did not know to what their suffering was due, they bowed their heads, as Job had done, to the will of God. As he, they

understood that the prosperity of evil people should
not shake ones confidence in God; as he, they expected salvation and help from God. It makes no difference that Job was slower in coming to resignation
and expected to gain insight on this earth. We
should however point out that the psalmists made
one important stride: they looked upon earthly
wealth not so much as a reward for a pious life,
but rather as toleration of the inveterate sinner who
could not expect anything more from life in the
hereafter.

2. Suffering and sin of the first man

We have seen that throughout the Old Testament
there is a tendency to explain suffering as punishment for a shortcoming, perhaps even an unknown
one, of forefathers, parents, a member of the clan,
the tribe or the town, the king or the person himself.
That Ezekiel, Job and a few psalmists[15] understood
this to be a very one-sided stance, especially concerning the collective aspect of the sanction and the
suffering of the just man, and that these authors
protested against this standpoint, is something which
does not concern us here.

Of course, this view had not just fallen from
space. Indeed we already find it in the first pages
of the Bible, and more especially in Gen. 3. There
we hear that man originally lived in communication
with God; but because of his disobedience he had to
leave the garden of Eden and settle on the face of the
earth which lay under God's curse — where suffering,

disease and death awaited him and his offspring, as
a punishment for the first sin. The story of Genesis
does not intend to stress that every man is a
sinner because of Adam's sin; it only means to point
out that Adam's sin is the cause of evil on earth.[16]

The standpoint of Genesis did not attain the
success we might expect it to have had: no commentary on this chapter is to be found until the 2nd
century B.C. At that time Ecclesiasticus, in a passage
against women, accuses Eve — not therefore Adam —
of having been the first one to sin and thus having
become the cause of death (Sir. 25, 23). Only in
the first century A.D. the apocryphal (!) apocalypses
of Baruch and Ezra once more point to Adam as the
cause of death.

In this connection it is noteworthy that according
to Gen. 3 the responsibility for the first sin and the
evil which ensued from it ultimately rests with
someone else, not with man. The serpent spoken of
there is not just an animal, it is the embodiment of
a being who seeks to create disorder, revolt and
pride, and therefore, by seducing man, tries to
thwart God's plan for mankind. But this aspect of
the question too did not attract attention for many
centuries, contrary to what we might have expected.
It is only in the first century B.C. that Wisdom gives
us this commentary: "But through the devil's envy,
death entered the world" (2:24).[17]

It is worthwhile to underline — in regard to what
might be called the theory of fate — that what we

have quoted never led to an inevitable conclusion: in stressing the connection between suffering and sin, the responsibility of man[18] was passed over in silence or minimized. What we have said in our first section has taught us the opposite.

Let us conclude with a short summary.

In the Old Testament suffering was not considered a kind of fate from which man was unable to escape[19]; it was considered a state of disorder brought about by sin. This might be the sin of others or of the person concerned. Sporadic stress was placed upon the devil's part in it. In both cases protests arose; especially in the last case there was resistance against the onesidedness of the current opinion. The result of it all was not that a rationally satisfactory solution was found, but that, in the strength of one's faith, one bowed one's head before the inscrutable wisdom and power of God.

B. THE MEANING OF SUFFERING

From what we have seen, we must distinguish between the meaning of collective and of individual suffering.

1. The meaning of collective suffering

Though the prophets were champions of religious individualism, and though their religious experiences and findings were the result of personal contact with Yahweh, they nevertheless looked upon Israel as one body.[20] Whatever they said about sin, punishment or salvation always pointed to Israel as such, often

personified as Yahweh's bride, the daughter of Jerusalem or the daughter of Zion, whose successive
generations are looked upon as solidary. Therefore
they spoke about "national" sin, which would be
followed by "national" punishment.[21] But they went
further. They saw punishment as part of the economy of salvation and they attributed to it a role
for conversion and atonement. They wished to
make people understand God's work in history, the
calamities of his approaching judgment; this purifies
and renews, so that God receives satisfaction and
reconciliation can be realized:

> Return, O Israel, to Yahweh your God,
> for you have stumbled because of your iniquity.
> Take with you words
> and return to Yahweh!

> Say to him:
> Take away all iniquity;
> accept that which is good
> and we will render
> the fruit of our lips.

> Assyria shall not save us,
> we will not ride upon horses;
> and we will say no more Our God to the work
>   of our hands;
> in thee the orphan finds mercy.

> I will heal their faithlessness;
> I will love them freely,
> for my anger has turned from them.
> I will be as the dew to Israel;
> he shall blossom as the lily.

He shall strike roots as the poplar;
his shoots shall spread out;
his beauty shall be like the olive
and his fragrance like Lebanon!

They shall return and dwell beneath his shadow,
they shall grow grain as a garden;
they shall blossom as the vine,
their fragrance shall be like the wine of Lebanon.

O Ephraim, what have I to do with idols?
It is I who answer and look after him.
I am like an evergreen cypress,
from me comes your fruit.

Whoever is wise, let him understand these
        things;
whoever is discerning, let him know them;
for the ways of the Lord are right,
and the upright walk in them,
but transgressors stumble in them!
     (Hos. 14:1-10; cf. 2; Is. 30; Jer. 24:7; 31:31-33).

It consequently became possible to look upon the
suffering which the people of God had to undergo
as a penance imposed by God; this was considered
necessary if Israel were to be preserved from total
destruction.[22] Whether people were aware of their
guilt or not was of little moment (cf. 2 Sam. 21).

The same type of reasoning occurs in the so-called
deuteronomic philosophy of history which marks
Deuteronomy, Joshua, Judges, Samuel, Kings and
Chronicles. This philosophy, proceeding from a

religious-pragmatic stance, usually followed a set pattern: infidelity of the people of God brings punishment; conversion brings prosperity and liberation. This has given scholars a reason to speak about "a religious pragmatism with four terms": national infidelity and punishment, national conversion and salvation.[23]

2. The meaning of individual suffering

Concerning individual suffering, the Bible makes a distinction between its effect on the community and its effect on the individual concerned.

a. The meaning of an innocent individual, suffering for the sinful community

One biblical figure comes to the fore in this connection: the suffering Servant of Yahweh.

Just as Jeremiah and Ezekiel do, the author of Deutero-Isaiah looks forward to the messianic time; he describes it as a period in which the Creator will lead his people to unexpected happiness and prosperity.[24] But he differs from these two prophets in that he sees not only Israel but other peoples as well sharing in the New Covenant: Sin has broken the relation between God and man, pagan as well as Jew; Ebed-Yahweh will restore it.[25]

More clearly than the two prophets did, this sacred writer throws a sharp light on the role of the Messiah in **conversion** and **redemption,** and his vision is largely new: return to God will come about through **vicarious suffering,** the sacrifice of life and

the atoning death of the suffering Servant who,
being himself without any guilt, will bear the sins
of all.[26]

This is the first and only time that suffering (and
moreover innocent suffering) of an individual is
described in the Old Testament as the one way to
atonement for the guilt of the world.

b. The meaning of an innocent individual, suffering for the guilty individual

Here we must first speak about the book of Wisdom. This shows clearly that in the first century
B.C. people had arrived at a clear insight into individual retribution in the hereafter. It was written in
Alexandria by a learned Jew; it shows traces of
hellenistic influence. The author says: When the
souls of the wise — the just — are liberated from the
burden of their bodies they go and dwell with the
Lord in his heavenly temple, where they share in
his reign (9:15; 3:9; 5:15; 3:14; 3:8; 5:6). Their happiness will consist of peace, love and knowledge; they
will reside in the midst of the saints or angels
(3:9; 5:5). On the other hand, the stupid — the sinners — will meet the tortures of Hades (4:9; 5:13).

Starting from this, the author of Wisdom resolutely
takes his stand concerning the suffering of pious men;
before his time this was a problem laden with
anxiety. Retribution, he argues, is not of an earthly
character; hence it does not matter at all whether
we live long, have few children or meet many diffi-
culties.[27] Can we say, for example, that a promising

young man dies too soon? No; this is evidence of
God's graciousness, because he puts this young man
at rest (4:7-8). Has someone few or many children?
It does not matter; an ungodly father of a large
family is not loved by God, while a eunuch and a
barren woman who fear God, are loved by him
(3:13-19; 4:1-6). Is our life on earth one series of
trials? It should be considered a purification bestowed upon us by Providence directing that a pious
man be made worthy of a happy life in the hereafter
(3:1-6, 9).

This kind of suffering is not meant to lead to conversion, expiation, atonement or reconciliation; but
it does appear to be **a necessary part of divine education.** It is a grace from God, which tries the pious
man as gold is tried in the crucible, in order to give
him a chance to prove his fidelity to God and thus
to opt for eternal happiness,[28] or to be protected
against the allurement of evil.[29]

c. The meaning of a guilty individual, suffering for the guilty individual

In 2 Sam. 7:14 we read "When he (Solomon) commits iniquity, I will chasten him with the rod of men,
with the stripes of the sons of men." Suffering is
here considered **a means to aversion from sin and
conversion to God,** so that **reconciliation** can take
place.

This reminds us of the prophetic preaching mentioned above in "The meaning of collective suffering." There we pointed out that the prophets were

thinking of the people collectively and that they
considered Israel as one body. This did not mean
that their exhortations for contrition, penance and
obedience to God are directed only to the nation
and not to every individual sinner in particular.[30]
Because they always opposed superficiality in cult
and ritual, they insisted upon moral and religious
conversion.[31] According to them, it was of utmost
importance to confess one's sins, to sin no more, to
renounce whatever separates one from Yahweh; to
redress social injustice; to confide in Yahweh's power
and fidelity; to go back to one's first love, Yahweh,
and relive with this first love the honeymoon of yore.
All these fruits they expected to result from suffering.[32]

Let us briefly summarize. God did not choose
individuals but a people; he willed to save the individual by incorporating him into that people.
Therefore the men of God tried their best to educate
Israel, Juda, the house of Jacob, the daughter of
Zion, the daughter of Jerusalem, the seed of Abra-
ham, the bride of Yahweh, the barren womb which
never bore children — all of these are expressions
meant to stress the idea of being a community.

Whenever the people of God proved untrue to
this choice, promise, covenant, circumcision and law,
the prophets based new expectations on suffering.
Guilty collective suffering, they said, is a judgment
of God which purifies and renews, so that God is
satisfied, and reconciliation can be realized. Of
course, this suffering had to be shared by all individ-

uals, not however as individuals — and therefore
regardless of personal guilt — but as members of
God's people; their sufferings had the value of a
penance imposed by God, which was necessary to
prevent Israel from being lost entirely. To the fore-
front came a figure who played the role of a collective person; his innocent suffering would be salutary
for Israel and for the rest of mankind, and his
death would be an atonement.

On the other hand, the suffering of an innocent
individual, considered in himself, was not part of
the atonement, but a necessary element in his education, helping him to reach God quickly and safely.

Further, a guilty individual's suffering was directed
to contrition, penance and obedience to God.

THE GRACE OF SUFFERING

In the New Testament we are on more familiar terrain. It is obvious that suffering here is seen explicitly and formally as a disorder caused by the sin of Adam — a disorder — weighing on every man, because every man shares in this sin of the first man.

"Therefore as sin came into the world through one man and death through sin, and so death spread to all men because all men sinned — sin indeed was in the world before the law was given, but sin is not counted where there is no law. Yet death reigned from Adam to Moses, even over those whose sins were not like the transgressions of Adam, who was a type of the one who was to come.

But the free gift is not like the trespass. For if many died through one man's trespass, much more have the grace of God and the free gift of grace of that one man Jesus Christ abounded for many. And the free gift in grace is not like the effect of that one man's sin. For the judgment following one trespass brought condemnation, but the free gift following many trespasses brings justification. If, because of one man's trespass, death reigned through that one man, much more will those who receive the abundance of grace and the free gift of righteousness reign in life through the one man Jesus Christ.

Then as one man's trespass led to condemnation for all men, so one man's act of righteousness leads to acquittal and life for all men. For as by one man's disobedience the many were made sinners, so by one man's obedience the many will be made righteous" (Rom. 5:12-19; cf. 3-23-26).

On the other hand, we should notice that the Old Testament problem was not yet entirely solved. Christ had to stress the fact that suffering is not necessarily a consequence of personal sins or of the sins of relatives and members of a group (Jn. 9:2-3). In this regard the doctrines of Jesus and Paul show an affinity with the words of Job (Mt. 26:36-46; 2 Cor. 12:7-10). But unlike Job they attribute a new significance to suffering, as does the oldest Christian kerygma. This significance does not simply coincide with the one of which we spoke above. They see suffering as a growing toward God rather than as an aversion from sin.

a. The meaning of Christ's suffering

Let us first point out that the suffering of Christ and of his followers is not necessarily a consequence of original sin, nor is it simply a punishment. It is chiefly governed by the law of a divine "must," but in such a way that the divine will to save mankind makes it a means of grace. Suffering therefore is not so much an aftermath of the first sin or a punishment for shortcoming, as it is the working out of God's economy of salvation.

This is evident from the prophecies and allusions regarding Christ's suffering, from the messianic mystery and from the parallelism existing between Jesus' suffering and the destiny of the Servant of Yahweh — a parallelism of which the synoptic tradition was well aware (Is. 53).[33]

The question of the salvific value of Jesus' suffering for every man in particular was not treated formally by the synoptics. But the elements of later answers to this question are already present in those texts where the atoning value and vicarious character of Jesus' passion are implicitly stated.[34]

In this connection the Acts speak in a language which is no clearer. There Jesus' suffering is often mentioned in texts which deal with the oldest Christian preaching, but its salvific value is not stressed; all the stress falls on its messianic value.[35] The Jews maintained that the Messiah could not and should not die, and that Jesus of Nazareth consequently could not be the Messiah. The Christians showed, Bible in hand, that he really was the Messiah, because he died as the prophets had foretold.[36] In their view, Christ's suffering was a successfully sustained trial imposed upon him by God, rather than an act of salvation; nevertheless the soteriological value is at least implicitly affirmed (Acts 3:15; 4:11-12; 8:32 in the light of Is. 53).

This soteriological value of Christ's passion is
expressed in a very clear way in the letters of Paul,
in Hebrews and the first letter of Peter.

Paul teaches that the figure of the suffering Servant of Yahweh was given form in Christ who suffered and died for the sins of all (Rom. 4:25). To
state this in our own words: By the vicarious suffering and the sacrifice of the Lord's life all men were
redeemed, reconciled with God, liberated from sin,
law, death and cosmic powers; thus he did everything
necessary to obtain from the Father the right to
found the Church and to distribute the grace of
salvation.

The cross and the scandal it aroused are placed in
the very center of his preaching: "For the word of
the cross is folly to those who are perishing, but to
us who are being saved it is the power of God" (1 Cor.
1:18). The cross also stands at the base of the
Christian cult: "Jesus, who, though he was in the
form of God, did not count equality with God a
thing to be grasped, but emptied himself, taking
the form of a servant, being born in the likeness of
men. And being found in human form he humbled
himself and became obedient unto death, even death
on a cross. Therefore God has highly exalted him
and bestowed on him the name which is above
every name, that at the name of Jesus every knee
should bow, in heaven and on earth and under the
earth, and every tongue confess that Jesus Christ is
Lord, to the glory of God the Father" (Phil. 2:6-11;
cf. 1 Tim. 1:16). The cross cannot be separated from

the sacramental event. As to this latter, Paul time and again argues that the suffering, death and resurrection of Jesus are not a kind of vessel from which one can draw endlessly, but rather a spring which keeps flowing and which pulses the vivifying waters through the channels of the Eucharist and Baptism.[37]

Paul considers the suffering and death of Jesus his greatest gesture of love.[38] To avoid misunderstanding we should stress that his vision of Jesus' suffering and death in no way denies that Christ was humiliated.[39] Nevertheless, and above all, it is a message of resurrection and life.

The letter to the Hebrews, it has been said, looks at the redemption as at a cultic drama. Christ is our High Priest, Mediator between God and mankind. Just as the levitic high priest carrying the sacrificial blood entered into the holy of holies in order to accomplish with it reconciliation, so also Christ entered into the heavenly sanctuary in order to offer to his Father his own blood. He died only once, but he continuously offers his blood to God.[40]

The first letter of Peter, using other terminology, develops the same thought. Here we read about the One who died for all — the just one for the unjust — who effected reconciliation through the power of his blood:

"For one is approved if, mindful of God, he endures pain while suffering unjustly. For what credit is it, if when you do wrong and are beaten for it you take it patiently? But if when you do right and suffer for it you take it patiently, you have God's approval. For to this you have been called, because Christ also suffered for you, leaving you an example, that you should follow in his steps. He committed no sin; no guile was found on his lips. When he was reviled, he did not revile in return; when he suffered, he did not threaten; but he trusted to him who judges justly. He himself bore our sins in his body on the tree, that we might die to sin and live to righteousness. By his wounds you have been healed. For you were straying like sheep, but have now returned to the Shepherd and Guardian of your souls" (2:1-25; cf. 1:1-18-19; 3:18).

Here too the theology of the cross is the foundation of the cult; not much attention is paid to the humiliation of suffering (1:18-21; 2:21-25; 3:18-22; 2:23).

b.   The meaning of suffering for a Christian

Early Christianity commonly held that persecution, hostility and resistance were essentially connected with its hope. They knew they had to suffer because Christ also suffered (Acts 4:23-30; 5:41; 9:5). Tribulations therefore were the sign that the messianic times had really arrived, that Christians shared in Jesus' suffering, and that sooner or later they would witness the Parousia. This induced them to consider the persecuted as saved and persecutors as condemned. In other words, they suffered with a certain hope of victory.[41]

There was another reason for their hope of victory: because of their tribulations the Holy Spirit poured joy and consolation into their hearts as a pledge and advance realization of the future joys (2 Cor. 1:3-7; cf. Acts 5:41).

In order to appreciate this to the full we should consider all the texts of Paul. According to Paul the life of a Christian is stretched between two poles: living and dying with Christ. Suffering therefore is not a privilege of the apostle or of certain Christians, but it belongs to the very essence of being a Christian; it even is a special grace, greater even than the grace of faith. Therefore Paul dares, without any fear of making a mistake, forewarn his Christian communities that trials await them. Suffering for him is not something which we merely bear; it is rather an active manly fight for the sake of Christ. Hence Paul too is not ashamed of his own suffering and he refuses to lose courage because of it. In the many hardships and trials and persecutions which Christians have to bear, he sees a reason for joy and happiness, a source of consolation, a real token of salvation and a pledge of security at the time of God's judgment.[42]

We find the same thought expressed in 1 Peter 2-5, where the author calls himself "a witness of the suffering of Christ" — a partaker of it; (5:1) and Hebrews teaches Christians that they are partakers of Christ and that their best help in suffering is the example of Christ (12:2-3; 2:10; 3:1, 14).

c. The meaning of suffering for a priest

Even more than in the suffering of the Christian, Christ's passion is continued in the suffering of his apostle, the priest.[43] Christ was afflicted and died, not for himself but for others. The same holds true for the priest; he too suffers, not primarily for himself but for others. The priest therefore has tribulations, not insofar as he is a follower of Christ (**because** Christ suffered) but insofar as he is a continuation of Christ (**in the same way that** Christ suffered). In other words, if one really is an apostle, a most important tool of Christ, he must undergo suffering and he must do so above all for others. If he does not do this or does not do it in this manner, or if he loses courage, he contradicts what he really is and at once becomes a sign of contradiction.[44]

This way of thinking in the letters of Paul originates from his conviction that he is the continuation of Christ as the suffering Servant of Yahweh according to the Deutero-Isaiah. We shall consider this more in detail, following relevant texts. The extent to which Paul's encounter with the risen Christ on the road to Damascus gave direction to his apostolate and to the lives of the people he met will become evident. Here we find the biblical foundation for the adage: "The priest is another Christ." This is true also in regard to his suffering. In Isaiah 49:1 we read of the vocation of the Servant of Yahweh: "The Lord Yahweh called me from the womb, from the body of my mother he named my name." This was for Paul the model of his own vocation. The choice and significance of his words in Gal. 1:15 show this. When we read this text it is evident that he was thinking about the terminology of Isaiah: "But when he who had set me apart before I was born, and had called me through his grace, was pleased to reveal his Son to me . . ." It is also evident that his thoughts too are inspired by Isaiah who taught that the vocation of the Servant had already been decided before his birth. An inaugurating vision made this vocation known to the person concerned. His activity was to have an influence on the gentiles. In the same way Paul mentions that God had already decided his vocation before his birth: "when he who had set me apart before I was born and had called me . . ." The introductory vision at Damascus did not intend to call him but to notify him of his vocation ("when he was pleased to reveal his Son to me"). His activity was to be directed to the gentiles ("When he . . . was pleased to reveal his Son to me, in order that I might preach him among the Gentiles").

This does not mean however that there are no points of difference. In Paul's case God took the initiative and Christ was the Mediator who notifies him of his vocation; Christ at the same time was the object of the task to which Paul was being called. Isaiah mentions that God took the initiative, but there is nothing about Christ. Next we note that "to reveal" is a technical term of apocalyptic writing; the vision on the road to Damascus therefore was an apocalypse: Paul saw the person of the risen and glorified Christ coming down to him, while God revealed that Jesus is his Son and therefore has the name "Son of God." Nothing of all this is found in Isaiah. From the Greek expression which we translate by "had set apart" it is evident that Paul, using Isaiah 49:1, has in mind more than a simple comparison between himself and the Servant. If we take this term in its full meaning it signifies "set apart and destined for." In Gal. 1:15 the term means that God had decided, before his birth, to charge him with the apostolate to the gentiles. And as this term is connected to Is. 49:1 Paul evidently expresses the conviction that he himself was prefigured in the prophecy about the Servant.

To put it precisely, we must add that Paul does not at all say that he himself is the Servant of Yahweh. Luke, who was his disciple and companion and therefore knew him from his doctrine and activity, designates Christ, not Paul, as the Servant. We read in Luke 2:33 that Simeon called Christ "A light for revelation to the Gentiles, and for glory to thy people Israel." This is nothing other than an application of Isaiah 42:6 to Christ: "I am Yahweh, I have called you in righteousness, . . . I have taken you (the Servant) by the hand and . . . given you (the Servant) as a covenant to the people (Israel), a light to the nations (gentiles)"; and Is. 49:6: "He (Yahweh) says: It is too light a thing that you should be my servant to raise up the tribes of Jacob and to restore the preserved of Israel; I will give you as a light to the nations, that my salvation may reach to the end of the earth." We see at once that, according to Luke, the prophecy about the Servant was entirely fulfilled in Christ. No other Servant of Yahweh can be expected. Jesus however stayed with the Jews and did not personally bring the light to the gentiles, as is evident from the course of his life. In Luke's opinion, judging from Acts 26:16-18 — and therefore also according to Paul's opinion — Christ, by order of God, handed over this part of his task to Paul, the apostle of the gentiles.

As to the practical realization of Paul's vocation, this follows from what we have said above that Paul will see it as an intervention of Jesus, the Servant, by order of God, and therefore as something belonging to the economy of salvation. There are other texts in which this is stated explicitly, especially 2 Cor. 6:1-2: "Working together with him (God), then, we entreat you not to accept the grace of God in vain. For he says: At the acceptable time I have listened to you, and helped you on the day of salvation. Behold, now is the acceptable time; behold, now is the day of salvation." The meaning is this: After having stated that God reconciled the world to himself in Christ and that he appointed the apostles to announce this message of reconciliation as legates of Christ, pleading his cause (5:19-20), Paul continues by saying that he himself is one of those cooperators with God, an emissary of Christ; and he exhorts the Corinthians not to neglect the grace, the acceptable time, the day of salvation (6:1; cf. Is. 49:8). These last words mean that the day of salvation has now dawned, because grace offers itself now at Corinth in Paul's preaching (6:2-4). We hear therefore that Paul was sent to the Corinthians by God as a representative of Christ. They were offered a special opportunity to obtain salvation, because at that moment Jesus, the Servant, was accomplishing his task in the person of Paul. In the words of Paul, Christ allowed them to partake of the grace of reconciliation, so that at that moment the eschatological judgment for them became a fact, favorable, and in advance. No text could give us a clearer insight into Paul's psychology as an apostle, as an "alter ego" or as a "prolongation" of Christ — another Christ.

Against the background of 2 Cor. 6:1-2 there are three other passages in the same letter which gain a surprising depth of meaning: 1:15-16; 1:18-22 and 2:14-17.

In 1:15-16 we read: "Because I was sure of this, I wanted to come first to you, so that you might have a double pleasure; I wanted to visit you on my way to Macedonia, and to come back to you from Macedonia and have you send me on my way to Judea." Paul here speaks about plans for his journey. For a long time he had wished to return to Corinth, in order to give them a double pleasure (literally, a second favor). In the light of 2 Cor. 6:1-2 "favor" does not mean that he wishes to give the Corinthians another proof of his friendship and care, but that his coming to them will be a means of procuring grace for them.

1:18-22 says: "As surely as God is faithful, our word to you has not been Yes and No. For the Son of God, Jesus Christ, whom we preached among you, Silvanus and Timothy and I, was not Yes and No; but in him it is always Yes. For all the promises of God find their Yes in him. That is why we utter the Amen through him, to the glory of God. But it is God who establishes us with you in Christ, and has commissioned us; he has put his seal upon us and given us his Spirit in our hearts as a guarantee." In order to defend his authenticity, Paul appeals to the divine veracity: as God fulfilled his promises of salvation in the person of Christ, so also he will fulfill his decision of Christianizing the Corinthians in the person of the apostle. The apostle therefore may not be suspected of instability, as he is a tool in God's hand. Moreover Paul preaches Christ, who made all the promises of God come true and who therefore is reliable. And if the object of Paul's preaching is reliable, then also his preaching itself is reliable — the more so because God has taken him into the community of Christ through the Holy Spirit. Paul therefore shares in the veracity of God and of Christ. A better argument is impossible. Corinthians therefore gives all possible assurance that Paul is not a double-edged sword. We should notice — this is our purpose — that Paul characterizes his preaching as saying "Yes" to God's plans for the Corinthians in virtue of Christ's presence in him. As once the preaching of Christ, so now the preaching of Paul is a great "Amen." By using this word Paul characterizes his preaching of the gospel as a

liturgical function, cultic action, which serves to
bring salvation by mediating between God and man.

Finally, 2:14-17 says: "But thanks be to God, who
in Christ always leads us in triumph, and through
us spreads the fragrance of the knowledge of him
everywhere. For we are the aroma of Christ to God
among those who are being saved and among those
who are perishing, to one a fragrance from death
to death, to the other a fragrance from life to life.
Who is sufficient for these things? For we are not,
like so many, peddlers of God's word; but as men
of sincerity, as commissioned by God, in the sight
of God we speak in Christ." The metaphors he uses
remind us of the ideas of the Ancients. They considered the scent of plants to be a material substance,
on which other plants, animals and men could
live, or from which they could die if it were poison-
ous. In the same way they thought that the mani-
festation of the Deity was accompanied by a delicious
fragrance (cf. Job 14:9; Sir. 23:15). Paul's description
presents Christ as a divine perfume, which must
spread its scent in order to bring about life. To
ensure this effect God uses the apostles. He puts
them on the plane of the perfume which is Christ,
so that through their mouths the sweet odor of
Christ might spread. In other words, it is Christ
who inspires Paul and who fills his words with the
odor of his presence. The consequence is that where
Paul speaks the listeners are made aware of Christ;
who has been destined for the fall and the rising of
many; they meet him in a prelude to his return at

the end of time and they are forced to choose to be with or against him.

The conclusion now is evident. Seeing the risen One and at the same time receiving a mission "makes" Paul an apostle. Seeing the glorified Christ is an eschatological event, by which he shares in a very special way in the glory and the power of the risen Redeemer and at the same time receives a mission in the name of God. When later he preaches, he is an orator rather than a commentator, more a man of authority and less a man of scriptural learning. This means that his words are a gift rather than an interpretation, more a judgment than an announcement.

We now know that Paul considered and expressed his conversion as a vocation which essentially included a mission to the gentiles, and therefore also included their vocation. His personal vocation and his knowledge of having been sent to the Gentiles had their origin in the revelation granted him on the road to Damascus (Gal. 1:15-16). We also know that he connected his vocation and its realization with the risen and glorified Christ (cf. Gal. 1:15-16 and 1 Cor. 15:1-8).

It would therefore contradict Paul's own testimony if we were to connect his vocation with his vision in the temple of Jerusalem, mentioned in Acts 22:17-21, even though some scholars think this should be done.[45] They hold that Paul was called as an apostle to the Gentiles not on the road to Damascus, but at Jerusalem; hence his missionary work in the

beginning followed the Jewish-Christian method: first
accepting Gentiles into the Jewish fold by adminis-
tering circumcision and by imposing the mosaic law
on them, later promoting them to Christianity. But
we insist: this does not agree with the texts and the
facts, as will be evident from what follows. We do
not assert that these scholars are altogether wrong.
We can ask ourselves moreover whether or not, or
if, at any time Paul changed his thinking in regard
to his vocation. It is true that in Gal. 1:15-16 and
in 1 Cor. 15:1-8 he solemnly declares the opposite
and that he never makes the slightest allusion to an
evolution in his thinking. But is all this in accord
with the truth? Personally, I think it is not. But I do
so for reasons other than those adduced by these
scholars. In spite of his positive statement that he
has been called as apostle to the gentiles during the
revelation near Damascus, it remains a fact that Paul
did not immediately and directly begin to preach
among the gentiles with all the authority which
later characterized him. We therefore have a right
to suppose that there was an evolution in his thinking and even in the clarity with which he understood
his own vocation. We may not forget that Paul was
a Jew and therefore shared all the common preju-
dices of his race, the more so because he was a
pharisee. Moreover, a certain amount of time is
required before a vocation can purify a man's mind
and heart entirely. Paul's evolution as apostle to
the gentiles is clearly shown in the manner in which
he reached the gentiles and preached the gospel to
them.

It is possible that Paul did not at once conceive the plan of founding churches consisting entirely of pagans. Originally he may have had a plan to form communities around a solid core of converted Jews — communities therefore of a Jewish-Christian type. This does not mean he made circumcision compulsory. The Greek expression in Acts 13:6 should not be translated "proselytes" but the "pious." So too the "devout converts to Judaism" in Acts 13:43 should be taken in a rather broad sense (cf. Acts 11:1-18). Later he changed his method. Luke situates this change at Antioch in Pisidia. Paul and Barnabas are asked to speak in the synagogue. Paul's homily is built entirely on the Jewish-Christian pattern; he speaks about Jesus as the Messiah of Holy Scripture. The hearers however abuse him and contradict him; he realizes that they reject the word of God. Consequently he resolutely turns to the pagans (Acts 13:16-49).

At the same time Paul changed his way of presenting the message of salvation: in Antioch of Pisidia it was still a Jewish-Christian message. At Lystra, during the same journey, it became universal in character: "And when the crowds saw what Paul had done, they lifted up their voices, saying in Lycaonian: The gods have come down to us in the likeness of men! Barnabas they called Zeus, and Paul, because he was the chief speaker, they called Hermes. And the priest of Zeus, whose temple was in front of the city, brought oxen and garlands to the gates and wanted to offer sacrifice with the people. But when the apostles Barnabas and Paul heard of it, they tore their garments and rushed out among the multitude, crying: Men, why are you doing this? We also are men, of like nature with you, and bring you good news, that you should turn from these vain things to a living God who made the heaven and the earth and the sea and all that is in them. In past generations he allowed all the nations to walk in their own ways; yet he did not leave himself without witness, for he did good and gave you from heaven rains and fruitful seasons, satisfying your hearts with food and gladness. With these words they scarcely restrained the people from offering sacrifices to them" (Acts 14:11-18).

We can therefore suppose there was an evolution in Paul's dealing with the pagans and in his method of presenting the gospel. But the texts do not allow us to say that he did not include pagans in his apostolate from the very beginning, without first making them proselytes to the Jewish religion. The fact that from the beginning he more or less followed the Jewish-Christian method does not mean that he was unaware of his vocation as apostle to the gentiles. Perhaps he thought that he carried out his mission sufficiently by going to the gentiles in the synagogue, making them "God fearing" — not proselytes — and later converting them to Christianity. The fact that he later changed this method may be explained as follows. He gradually noticed that the Jews were more and more deserted by God, while the pagans in great numbers were converted to faith in Christ. Therefore he ultimately went directly to the pagans. It seems reasonable to allow him a certain time for learning from experience.

Thus, through the interaction of the vision on the road to Damascus, from repeated reading of the prophecies about the suffering Servant of Yahweh and from his practical experience, Paul realized to the full what his mission as an apostle to the gentiles really meant, even though this image had already been present from the time of Damascus as an invisible stamp. Certainly, in Gal. 1:15-20 he says: "When he who had set me apart before I was born, and had called me through his grace, was pleased to reveal his Son to me, in order that I might preach him among the Gentiles, I did not confer with flesh and blood, nor did I go up to Jerusalem to those who were apostles before me, but I went away into Arabia; and again I returned to Damascus. Then after three years I went up to Jerusalem to visit Cephas, and remained with him fifteen days. But I saw none of the other apostles except James the Lord's brother. In what I am writing to you, before God, I do not lie!" But this does not mean that he had nothing in common with the Jewish-Christian method of preaching the faith. It means only that he did not simply copy this method, that he did not circumcize pagans first and baptize them later.

Let us conclude with a short summary.

In order to help the world, God made Christ's suffering a vicarious suffering and his death an

atoning death. For man this vicarial aspect does not
mean that henceforth he does not have to suffer
himself; it means that in his suffering the suffering
of Christ is repeated and continued. Suffering for
him therefore is not a curse but a blessing, an encounter with and a merging into the Redeemer. It
therefore ought not be a source of sadness and
rebellion and it should not induce us to develop an
inferiority complex. It must be made a cause for joy.
Moreover, especially for the priest, it is a manly
combat for the sake of Christ and the redemption
of the world.

GENERAL CONCLUSION

Professor G. Verbeke of Louvain University writes
in his interesting book **The Mystery of Hope:** "There
are people who have no hope. Schopenhauer said
that to him human existence looked like a series
of disappointments. Franz Kafka, who had con-
siderable influence on contemporary thought, sees
man as a convict who is condemned to death,
but who does not know the facts of the case on
which his condemnation was based. He does not
know why he has to die or what the crimes are of
which he is accused; the whole procedure is not
clear to him: it is a senseless sequence of formalities
whose meaning he does not understand. Albert
Camus sees man engaged in a quest of the unattain-
able; the growing experience of life teaches him that
his deepest aspirations never will be fulfilled. This
is the great discovery which we find in his **Caligula:**
a gradually growing awareness of the meaningless-

ness of existence. All this points to a kind of devaluation of existence. It is no longer considered a gift of God, a boon of God's graciousness, a blessing which forms the base of all other benefits . . . The hopeless devaluation of human existence very evidently and continuously finds expression in birth-control: This is only understandable from a philosophy of life in which the horizon of existence is placed within the earthly life. People see only a chain of events of life and arrive at a pessimistic hopelessness . . . It seems doubtful to them whether it is advisable to bring new human beings into existence, because life is seen as a laborious journey toward an unknown destination.

According to modern thought, man lives his existence in loneliness: he alone is responsible for it and he can rely only upon himself. One can not fall back upon other people: each man lives his own existence, in an invincible solitude. He is shut up within himself, in the unique originality of his own intimacy; others have no access to it . . . Neither can man rely upon God; one knows nothing about his existence. Man therefore is a deserted being at each moment of his existence . . . Hence the hopelessness which weighs him down when he becomes aware of his dereliction.

How different is the message of the Bible!

Though it is two or three thousand years older, when compared with modern thought it still has a new ring to it; it can inaugurate a new spring if

man has the courage to believe and to hope even
though he suffers or one might better say, because
he suffers.

One who suffers is continuously inclined to ask
himself: Why? He will not find in the Bible a rational
answer which satisfies him. But he may be induced
by the holy pages to consider suffering as a state
of disorder, called into being by sin. At the same
time he will understand that it is not a catastrophe
brought about by blind fate but an arrangement of
the inscrutable wisdom of God, before which he has
to bow his head in the strength of his faith.

In the strength of his faith he will become aware
that suffering is not revenge, not a counter-measure
of the Deity against him in order to show him his
place and to settle accounts with him. Suffering
is always meaningful, whether a man is a sinner or
not. Its aim is that humanity, with which every
man is solidary, will not lose its eternal happiness;
it exhorts the sinful individual to turn away from
sin and convert himself to God, while for the just
man it is a necessary element of divine education.

Christ's suffering effects that man's suffering be
able to do all this. The Son of God suffered for all;
and after his ascension his suffering continues in the
suffering of man. Man therefore never suffers alone:
he suffers also, and at the same time, for others.
Suffering already contains within itself the effects
which make it a source of consolation and joy.[46]

NOTES

1. See Ps. 88:13; Job 10:21-22; Ps. 95:17; Job 7:9-10; **38:17;** Ps. 9:4.

2. See Ps. 6:6; 88:11-13; 115:17; Eccles. 9:5-6; Job 14:20-22.

3. See Ps. 13:4; 28:1; Job 3:13, 17-19; 7:15.

4. E.g. Gen. 34; Josh. 7:24-25; Num. 16:32; 2 Sam. **3:29; 24.**

5. Job 4:7; 7:8; 15:4, 17, 18; 18; 20:4.

6. See Gen. 4:10; cf. 37:26; Is. 26:21; Ezek. 24:8.

7. See Ps. 102:1; cf. Ps. 79:11; 88:3; Lam. 3:44.

8. See Job 19:10; 20, 22; 30:13, 18, 30; 33:21, 22-30.

9. See Job 7:9; 10:21; 14:7-22; 16:22.

10. See Job 3:17-19; 7:9, 10, 15; 10:21-22; 38:17.

11. "It" means that evil people prosper and the good are afflicted.

12. The end of the evil people.

13. In order to redeem oneself from death.

14. Because of the earthly happiness of sinners.

15. The Book of Wisdom will be treated later.

16. Therefore there is no question of "original sin" nor of suffering as "a consequence of original sin": "The doctrine of original sin is a Christian doctrine which the Old Testament only suggests in a very wide sense" says

M. J. Lagrange in a text quoted by A. Gelin, *Les idées
maîtresses de l'Ancien Testament,* coll. *Lectio Divina,*
y. 2, Paris 1955, p. 69.

17. The devil (in Hebrew *Satan*) is in the heavenly court as
the adversary of man. Being the angel of destruction,
he is the adversary of man rather than the enemy of
God: it is he who humiliates Job in God's eyes and who
brings David to sin (Job 1:6-12; 1 Chron. 31:1; Rev.
12:9). Jewish tradition identifies him with the snake
of paradise (Rev. 12:9) and gives him names such as
Azazel and Belial, which originally were names of evil
spirits.

18. The responsibility about which we speak here (for the
sake of clarity we repeat this) is the responsibility of
man in the person of his forefathers or parents, of a
member of his clan, tribe or city, of the king or in his
own person.

19. To this remark we might add: In the time of paradise
man did not know suffering (Gen. 1) and in the beatific
end-time there will no longer be place for suffering
(Is. 65:16-18; 66:22; Rev. 21:1). It is therefore wrong to
speak about fatalism.

20. The explanation of this paradox, it seems to us, should
be found in a decision of God's salvific will rather than
in a kind of conservatism: on the level of religion the
sense of solidarity should remain, surely in an ever
increasing purified form, in view of the salvation of
Christ, which brought salvation to man by incorporating him into the community of God's children.

21. As to this "national sin" cf. e.g. Is. 6:5; Jer. 5:1-2;
6:28-29; 7:29; 13:23; 1 :11-12; 17:1-2; Ez. 2:3; 16; 24; 1
Kings 8:46; Deut. 2:12; 4:25-28; 9:6; 32:5, 29; Num. 32;
13; As to "national punishment" cf. Hos. 5:4-9; 9-14;
7:10-12; 11:1-7; Amos 4:6-11; Is. 2:6-22; Zeph. 1:14-18;
Jer. 15:4; 24:18-10; 26:6; 29:18; 44:12; Joel 2:1-2; Deut.
4:26; 9:4.

22. We say ". . . if Israel were to be preserved from **total** destruction," because not every individual would **come** to conversion; many would continue in their evil ways and thus would continue downward in their obduracy. Suffering therefore would affect the so-called "small remnant" of Israel (cf. the story of Noah and **the** questions of Eliah, Amos, Hosea, Isaiah, Micah, **Jere-** miah, Zephaniah, Ezekiel, Joel, Obadiah and **Malachi;** cf. Rev. 9:20-21; 16:9, 11).

23. See e.g. Deut. 4:29-40; 5:29; Josh. 1:1-9; 7; **23:2-16;** 24:1-28; Judg. 1:6; 3:8; 1 Sam. 12:9-11; 1 Kings 11:9-13; 2 Kings 17:7-23; 18:5; 22:18-22; 2 Chron. 27:6; **28:19.**

24. See Is. 51:1; 52:12 and 54:5-17 with Jer. **31:31-33;** 33:15-16, 25-26 and Ezek. 11:19-20; 18:31-32; **36:26.**

25. See Is. 42:6, 7; 7:17-25; 49:6; 52:13-15; 54; **55:3b-5.**

26. See Is. 42:1-7, 46:12-13; 49:5-13; 52:13; 53:12; cf. **24:23;** 7-12.

Wisdom 4:7-18

But the righteous man, though he die early, will **be** at rest.
For old age is not honored for length of time,
nor measured by number of years;
but understanding is gray hair for men,
and a blameless life is ripe old age.

There was one who pleased God and was loved **by** him,
and while living among sinners, he was taken **up.**
He was caught up lest evil change his understanding or guile his soul.
For the fascination of wickedness obscures what is good,
and roving desire perverts the innocent mind.
Being perfected in a short time, he fulfilled **long** years;
for his soul was pleasing to the Lord,

therefore, he took him quickly from the midst of
    wickedness.
Yet the peoples saw and did not understand,
nor take such a thing to heart,
that God's grace and mercy are with his elect,
and he watches over his holy ones.

The righteous man who has died and will condemn
    the ungodly who are living,
and youth that is quickly perfected will condemn
    the prolonged old age of the unrighteous man.
For they will see the end of the wise man,
and will not understand what the Lord purposed for
    him,
and for what he kept him safe.
They will see, and will have contempt for him,
but the Lord will laugh them to scorn.
After this they will become dishonored corpses.
and an outrage among the dead forever.

Wisdom 3:1-6; 9.

But the souls of the righteous are in the hand of God,
and no torment will ever touch them.
In the eyes of the foolish they seemed to have died,
and their departure was thought to be an affliction,
and their going from us to be their destruction;
but they are at peace.
For though in the sight of men they were punished,
their hope is full of immortality.
Having been disciplined a little, they will receive
    great good,
because God tested them and found them worthy of
    himself;
like gold in the furnace he tried them,
and like a sacrificial burnt offering he accepted them.

Those who trust in him will understand truth,
and the faithful will abide with him in love,
because grace and mercy are upon his elect,
and he watches over his holy ones.

28. See Wisd. 3:5, 6, 9; 4:2, 15.

29. See Wisd. 4:10-14; 3:5-6, 9; cf. Ps. 16; 49; 73; Job 32-37; Prov. passim.

30. The deuteronomic tradition directs itself not so much to groups as to individuals.

31. It was not sufficient, they said and repeated, to be a pillar of the sanctuary, a specialist in sacrificing, a star in doing penance! See Amos 3:14-15; 4:4-5; 5:21-25; Mic. 6:6-8; Hos. 4:4-10; 5:1-7; 6:1-11; 7:13 - 8:3; 10:1-8; 12:12; 13:1-3; Is. 1:11-20; 58:2-7, 9; Jer. 21-23; 14:10-12.

32. See Jer. 3:13; 15:7; 18:11; 23:14-21; 25:5; 35:15; Ezek. 6:3-10; 36:31-32; Amos 8:4-14; Is. 1:11-31; Is. 8:16-17; 9:10-12, 27; 30:15-26; 31:1-6; Hos. 2:9, 16, 21-22; 6:1-3; 8:13; 9:3; 14:2-4; Jer. 3:19-22; cf. Jer. 4:4-31; 9:24-25; 11:15-16; 31:18-34; 32:36-44; Ezek. 36:22-36.

33. Mk. 8:31; 9:31; 10:33-34; 8:12; 9:15; 12:38; 26:18; Mk. 10:38; Lk. 12:50; Mt. 12:16-21; Mk. 9:29-30; Lk. 9:18-22; cf. Mt. 8:16 with Is. 53:4; Mt. 20:28 and Mc. 10:45, and 14:24 with Is. 53:10; Mk. 9:12-13 with Is. 54:3; Mk. 10:45 and 14:24 with Is. 53:11-12; Mk. 28-29 and Lc. 22:37 with Is. 53:12.

34. See e.g. Mk. 10:15 and 14:24 as read in the light of Is. 53:12; cf. also the theme of John: Jesus the light of the world. the idea the Redeemer of the world, in Jn. 17:19.

35. As to the Jews: see Acts 2:23-36; 3:15; 4:10; 5:30; as to the pagans see Acts 13:17-41; 17:3; 26:23.

36. The salvific value was attributed to the resurrection.

37. See 1 Cor. 10:16; 11:23-29; Rom. 6; Col. 2:12; Eph. 5:25; cf. Jn. 7:37-39.

38. See Gal. 1:14; 2:10; 2 Cor. 5:14; Rom. 5:8; Eph. 5:2, 25.

39. See 1 Cor. 1:25; 2 Cor. 13:14.

40. See Hebr. 3:1; 4:14; 8:1; 9:21; 5:1; 9:7; 4:14; 6:19; 9:24; 9:12; 12:24; 9:28.

41. See Acts 4:23-30; 5:41; 9:5; 1 Thess. 1:3; 2:13-16; 2 Thess. 1:4-10; Rom. 5:3-5.

42. See Ph.il 1:29; 2 Tim. 3:13; Acts 14:22; 1 Thess. 3:3; 2 Tim. 1:12; Eph. 3:13; 2 Cor. 12:7; 2 Cor. 8:2; Col. 1:24; Phil. 2:17; 2 Cor. 7:6; Phil. 1:28; 2 Thess. 1:4-5.

43. We must say the same about the resurrection of Christ, which repeats and manifests itself in the fortitude of the priest in spite of adversity and adversaries.

44. See 2 Thess. 1:10; Gal. 1:16; 4:19; 2 Cor. 1:5-7; 4:4b-6, 10-12; 5:20; 12:7-10; 13:4; Col. 1:24; 2 Tim. 9-10.

45. A. Fridrichsen, *The Apostle and his Message,* Uppsala, 1947.

46. Literature consulted: J. Schneider, *Die Passionsmystik des Paulus,* Leipzig, 1929; G. Wencke, *Paulus über Jesu Tod,* Gütersloh, 1939; H. Braun, "Das Leiden Christi: eine Bibelarbeit über den 1 Petri" *(Theol. Exist. heute 69,* 1940); Th. C. Vriezen, *Hoofdlijnen der theologie van het Oude Testament,* Wagningen, 1949; H. N. Ridderbos, *De komst van het koninkrijk,* Kampen, 1950; M. Meinertz, *Theologie des N.T.,* Bonn, 1950; J. Heuschen, "Lijden," in *Bijbels Woordenboek 2* Roermond-Maaseik, 1954-1957; N. Greiteman - G. Bouwman, "Hebreenbrief," ibidem; J. A. E. van Dodewaard - J. Heuschen, "Verzoening," ibidem; G. Verbeke, *Het mysterie van de Hoop,* Brugge, 1960.